UNSAID WORDS OF AN INDIAN GIRL

MARILYN JAIN

Contents

Preface

Enter Caption

Never really understood, why everyone hated girls so much! What we did that made people so angry? And I still don't understand, I always wanted answers but never got any.

I wrote this book on the behalf of every single female in India, From the experiences of what we heard and suffered, For the women who never had a voice, for that unborn little angel, For those who were raped but never served justice, For every single girl that wished to be born as a boy.

CHAPTER ONE

WELCOME, GIRL!

"Why name me if you never wanted me to exist?
Why made me live if you wanted me to die?
I would have been happier if you never had me!
I am sorry if I did something wrong
But this ain't the punishment I deserved"

'Congratulation, It's a girl.', they said.

Silence spread everywhere and in no time everyone started grieving. Some said, 'don't worry, it will be better next time.' Some said, 'It's your fate, you have to accept it.'

It all seemed fine when some said, 'KILL HER.'

Whenever a girl is born, the majority of people grieve, even their parents. Some of those newborns don't even make it a single day and are murdered by their parents or family members. And the story ends there.

We say that it's good that they are dead and in heaven now because those who live have to go through hell.

Even though sex determination is prohibited in India, there are a lot of places where it's done illegally, and if it appears to be a female, it takes no time for them to abort the pregnancy.

That first cry cost her everything. Her appearance makes the world criticise the person who gave her birth. Everyone who saw her made a face like they saw disgust.

There are several traditions, more like a celebration in India, to be performed when a child is born. It's like a joyous celebration of the arrival of a newborn. We see those happy faces all around, but under one condition, it must be a BOY. If it's a girl, there won't be any of those.

People even hesitate to congratulate the parents, because for them it is not a matter of joy, but grief.

The only reason why a boy is like an investment in their future is that he will grow to work and earn to feed the family. Still, on the other hand, if you raise a girl, it's just a waste of money, because she will marry and spend the rest of her life with another family and doing stuff for the other family.

This mindset of people never changed.

And the saddest part is that even females have this mindset. I don't get it, if we females can't support other females, then who will?

A lot of times, parents abandon her, leave her in the temple, on the street, or in an orphanage, and most of the time the child doesn't survive.

Sometimes they give them to their relatives to take care of them, it might have been for a good reason, but their life ends up being terrible most of the time, and sometimes even good, but the good part is very rare to happen.

Mostly in villages and small towns, the custom of child marriage is so intense that they might fix it at the moment they are born. This has changed a lot, to be honest, but much work is needed there.

A child is a child, we are the ones telling them their gender, raising them the 'WAY' they are supposed to according to their gender. Children become what we teach them, what thoughts we introduce to them, and what surroundings we give them. We should be happy when a child is born regardless of the gender, it's a life that made it through the gestation period and is finally here to live!

We shouldn't be the ones to impose our practices, and ideas on them.

They need to explore and find themselves in this world.

No boundaries, no restrictions, do what they like, a child won't go bad, I promise.

But we do need to understand and give it a try, we never know what children have in themselves that never comes out due to the restriction of things because their 'Gender' won't allow it.

Enter Caption

CHAPTER TWO

TODDLE OODDLE...

Enter Caption

"The day I spoke my first word, I was silenced.
The day I took my first step, I was put in a wheelchair.
Those all firsts I had were beautiful,
But I never knew my wings were about to be clipped.

Whenever a child turns into a toddler, a new world opens for them to explore, to learn.

Every kid gets excited when they see new things, they start walking and speaking, and they are kinda getting independent in some way.

But here's when things start to turn around for her, people around her start to interrupt anything she may do, even the smallest.

Every day is a war for that kid, people coming and suggesting their parents start saving money for her marriage, don't educate her, don't give her much cause it's just a girl.

I have seen people making their daughter sleep on the floor, not putting her in the room where it's air-conditioned, not making her drink milk or eat fruits or veggies which are pretty important for her growth, not taking her for an outing, and not buying clothes for her

And they even do all these things to her, just because if got married in a poor household these things will affect the groom's family it's of no use as it's a girl, she doesn't need anything

WHY?

That little girl is the victim of discrimination from the moment she can remember being alive, every person is preferred over her in every situation you can think of. And the only thing they have to say after being asked why they did that is, "it's a girl, why does she want all that stuff". This is awful, if you think it's important for a boy, it's also important for a girl too. Even though efforts are being made for the improvement of females in India, change has been seen, drastic ones, but a huge number of the population is still stuck with the thought of inferior and superior gender.

For a child, toddlerhood is the foundation of their character, interests, and limitations. At this tender age, they learn a lot, from seeing us or figuring it out themselves. This is the age they will establish a picture of how the world works. And this is the age where most of us don't care what we are doing around them, we neglect it as if they don't understand, but it's a myth, toddlers get way more out of the talk than we think they do.

Have you ever noticed, A child being so rude to their mother and not their father? Showing respect to the males around them but not to the females? Seeing the surroundings to talk to a male if they need to argue but never bothering if it would have been a female? Feeling inferior and not stepping up for themselves? Seeing males as a superior gender, and mocking others.

And all these questions aren't just about boys, but every child.

Have you never noticed any of these? Well, I have.

I feel sorry for the parents but at some point, it's their fault. Where would a child have learned all this? Their home!

Directly or indirectly it's always the fault of the grown-ups around that kid. A kid doesn't know all this crap. We made it all and now we are passing it on, knowing that it doesn't make any sense.

If you don't want your kid to be the person who once bullied you, give them an environment in which there is no sexism, no racism, no biased opinions, but, freedom, and open-mindedness.

Teaching your kid to respect everyone they meet, to be polite, and not think of anyone as inferior is the least you could do to make that young fella into a great human being.

This phase of a child is to learn, and that learning should be appropriate to mold them into good beings.

CHAPTER THREE

Real World Awaits!

Enter Caption

"Everyone looked at me with keen eyes
As if I did something bad
Everything seemed right, Everything seemed wrong
Was it me or the fear of me growing?
Still, I am confused!"

Adolescence is a power pack of emotions, hormones, growing up, and understanding, it's quite a lot to cope with. It brings a lot of responsibilities, teens are asked to act like adults but are treated like children.

Teenage is different for different people, but when it comes to the account of females in India, there can't be any other common ground. Problems they went, all that hustle, and the way how everything suddenly changes for them.

Growing up is weird. Everything changes, friends, family, you, everything! Hormones tease you. You're converting into something you always wanted, but still, you fear it.

For a girl growing up is special, only till society lets it. Girls experience the development of breast, widening of the pelvic region, and more, these changes are to be embraced, but for some, these changes impact the confidence of a girl, maybe because not being introduced to the right garments or the way people starts looking at them.

Some families make her wear a lot of clothes to cover it up, and I don't blame them because they are trying to protect them, but instead, she loses all their charm and, her confidence is lowered to a great extent. An inferiority complex is built within that person.

Most teens especially girls get Body shamed; ***their height, weight, color, size of their bust and buttocks, face, and every single body part!***

It hurts even more when I see women body shaming! If a female can't support another female I don't other gender supporting her. As a female one should support her fellow females, no matter what.

If we want to bring a change, we got to start by changing ourselves.

That First Day (shh!)

Enter Caption

Let's start with the thing that marks the start of a teenage, ***"Her first period"***. Talking about menstruation openly is considered as you did something illegal, or to say it otherwise people think it is embarrassing to talk about periods, and just for no reason.

Most adolescent girls or the girls who are about to enter their adolescence are not taught anything about periods. Even when a girl gets her first period, most Indian girls don't what just happened to them.

Let's take an example, A girl returns home from her school, and immediately she enters the changing room, she pulls down her pant and sees blood! Frightened from the inside, not knowing what to do, she just sat there for a while.

The example taken above can end in various ways, she doesn't tell anyone changes into her casual clothes, thinking that she is dying or something, and is so helpless at the moment. Another can be she goes to anyone at her home, trying to figure out what is wrong with her.

Whatever the scenario may be, not knowing what just happened, seeing blood from a very sensitive part of the body, and all that PMS! A girl goes through so much in that little period, she is clueless, frightened, helpless, in pain, and even so much that can't be explained.

And when they do understand what periods are, they are taught that age-old myths about periods that when heard make no sense at all. Some of them are like:-

-Don't enter the temple

-Don't touch the pickle

-Sit outside the house

-Don't take a bath

-Don't touch plants

-Don't eat sour foods

This list just has some common myths, but there is a lot more that surrounds a female during her period, every region and culture has its own sets of myths.

It is believed that a woman is impure and is considered dirty just because she has a menstrual flow, period blood is considered impure and if u ask someone for a logical reason behind it, I can bet no one can give any. How is period blood impure?

If period blood is impure then that makes every single human on this planet impure!

We are making good progress in normalizing period talk and busting the myths, but there is a lot more we need to do, all that progress but only a few people have access to it.

Still, in many rural areas, women don't have access to sanitary pads or tampons, instead, they use old clothes and other unhygienic things, which when used for a long time can cause serious health issues, the lack of awareness, the shame they feel to ask about sanitary pads, may be one of the many reasons. Only 20% of women in India use sanitary pads, tampons, or menstrual cups.

Menstrual cups brought a great revolution, they are eco-friendly, budget-friendly, and above all, it's the most comfortable among all the products available. Besides all its advantages, Indian households developed a stereotype for menstrual cups, "You'll lose your virginity if you use a menstrual cup" which is so NOT true.

Losing virginity and breaking the hymen are two different things! Hymen can break during vigorous exercise or running at a very young age, but that doesn't mean the girl lost her virginity.

When the girl loses her virginity, people starts seeing her as dirty, impure and mocking her daily basis! Why it's wrong for a girl lose her virginty, If she was aware and it was her will, ***There is nothing wrong with it.***

Society has created a very unsafe environment for menstruators, teens, and working women to spend most of their day at school or the office respectively, and if they get their period at school, they are made fun of, and people who do are boys or men who are not taught about periods like man seriously you are a product of missing a period, if your mother never got her first period, you wouldn't sitting here laughing.

And it's not just boys, the teachers and bosses if they find a stain on a girl's uniform or her clothes, they'll gossip about it in the staff room and accuse the girl that her mother didn't teach her to wear a pad, and that breaks a person from inside.

And her fellow girls, some of them are helping but some are so mean, that they form a group and starts making fun of her.

Periods are normal, stains are normal, forgetting your cycle is normal, and making fun and harassing someone for something as normal as breathing is something only a person with a conservative mindset will do, and sadly that's half of India!

A girl needs comfort, safety, and warmth in the environment during her periods, she is the most vulnerable at the time, and she needs to be taken care of, but that's not the case in India, knowing that the girl is on her period, everybody starts to act weird, and they all treat her as if she has committed a crime.

The change is there but let's make it a change everybody can see and enjoy.

Rape Culture

Enter Caption

Rapes are a huge problem in India. People believe that wearing short clothes is the main reason why the rate of rapes has increased in India; What is wrong with people? Daily, we hear about a huge of rape cases, which include girls of age merely some months to old women,

So was that little girl wearing short clothes and that 'excited' people and got raped?

No! Clothes don't matter! People who rape are monsters!

We got to teach young children to respect others and teach them forcing someone is not good.

Stereotypes of why rapes happen are:-

-Going out or staying outside till late at night

-Talking and being friendly with males

-The way one dresses

-Laughing loudly

-or standing up for yourself, etc.

Yeah, I know what you are thinking, all the above examples make no sense at all! but all these do prevail in India as the main reason for rapes. and just because of all of this; their families sets curfews and obligations for a girl, but not for the boy.

Victims of rape are not just females; more than half of rape case victims are young boys and men, but the thing is most of these rapes do not make it to the police station, or even if they do, there are no media that will cover the story.

The main reason why we don't hear about these rapes is due to the shame the victim's family feels! Why u feel ashamed, your kid didn't do anything wrong, they deserve justice, and saying reporting it will bring shame to the family, you are just taking them away from themselves

I have heard people rubbish about males being raped, like'

"It's not even biologically possible for a male to get raped, it doesn't make any sense"

"It's not rape when it's male"

The term rape is not specified for just females or males, Rape is Rape!

Rapists sometimes may be stranger, but sadly, for most of the cases that we see, the rapist is someone very close to the victim, their uncle, aunt, step-parent, grandparent, friend, or even their biological parent!

Seeing this, where is that Indian culture that we brag about, that *integrity, purity* of the relations we talk about, Where is it? The monster is in the house, and we are afraid of sending our loved ones outside! wow!

Torture isn't done yet, that person got raped, is weak and in pain both mentally and physically, and then our beloved society comes to play their role and that is to ***slut-shame, and sympathize*** the victim.

Things that a person gets to hear after this traumatic event, break them. There is no one to support or who understands, everyone has their own opinion:-

-Now, who will marry him/her? (mostly her)

-He/she is impure

-They spoiled the family's reputation, etc

What's the fault of the victim? What did they do wrong? How are they impure?!

Victims of rape are ***sexually objectified***, people stop respecting them, and give them a disgusting look.

Not reporting Rape, is mainly because the family and victim don't want to go through all the societal torture, and this is Bad. You are basically letting that rapist, that monster be free and commit more rapes, more innocent people will be victims! and more people will believe committing rape is fine, as nobody is going to say anything.

Please report! Whether it's someone close to you, someone, you know, someone you just met, or if that someone is YOU. Everybody needs justice and this ***Brutal*** crime needs more than just justice.

RAPE IS NOT FINE!

CHAPTER FOUR

HEART HARDENS

Enter Caption

Society continues to be as it was before, and now it even gets worse, the whole world is waiting for that little girl, who is now grown up to step in so that they treat her even worse.

But this time, they don't know that she is prepared! She knows what she has to face, she knows that the world won't change for her, instead, she has ***TO BE THAT CHANGE!***

With all that great milestones to archive, comes that pointless burdens from society, family, friends, and colleagues.

With every step takes, she has to prove that is capable, she is *Worth it.*

And I must say I truly respect you!

Women with this mindset are the only ones that in the end may be happy with how their life turned out. But sometimes it gets hard for a woman to go against their family and society, as she has always been suppressed!

But I still think you don't have a slave to someone, you got to stand up for yourself, you deserve so much better and you have to do that for yourself, Girl!

Blaming people for how your life turned out, how everyone treated you, how they said NO! It isn't the solution! You got one life, and whenever you start taking charge, A new phase, A new world will open for you! No matter how much you have aged, no matter how low you feel, one day you have to be ***who you are!***

Every aspect of life contains more than one scenario and so does here; It all starts when a girl is at the end of her high schooling, and that girl is merely 18 years of age, and taking into account here I talk about the majority of India, even before 12th class board exams, her family starts looking for a boy to marry her. and at the moment of time, and just after her exams, before the result is declared, her title goes from ***Miss. to Mrs. Unkown.***

That was an example, but truth for half of the housewives in India. Every woman in India at some point in her life is forced by her family and relatives to marry some random guy! She doesn't get to pick who will be her partner.

However, may that random guy and his family may treat her, *She has to remain silent!* You know why, because that isn't '*Her home*' and that so-called '*Her home*' isn't her home either!

For women to have a job in India, is difficult, both in the matter of the workplace and their families. when a woman wants to work she has to take 'permission' either from her husband, father, or brother! And the reason remains unknown, but still, they have to, and when she doesn't she is said to be rebellious! What kind of system is this?

She is an adult and has the full right to make her own decisions, She is not obligated to anyone!

And when it comes to the workplace, male supremacy prevails there! Her pay is lower than males for the equal amount of work, She is treated with inferiority, and all that just because, *she is a female.*

Things don't end there, she has to go through troubles on a daily basis.

Molestation, where do I even start, wherever you go see someone being molested, and yet we don't do anything, because we don't want to go trouble ourselves. Workplace, bus, train, park, and everyplace u can think of, but she is even ***molested in her own house.***

When a girl marries a guy, and at some point, she thinks that he might be good, will treat her good, but No! I know some do treat her good and support her, but that ratio!

That guy she just married, and she is bonded with him for life! he treats her like a slave, she has to do all chores and ask his permission for doing literally anything.

She is raped every night by her own husband! Most of the kids in India are the products of marital rape!

She is forced by everyone to have a baby! They don't care about her will, her work. but when it comes to Him, his work is really important! And when she does get pregnant, she is treated like hell, what an irony!

But she bears everything! And by now she is used to it!

CHAPTER FIVE

IF LIFE COULD BE RE-LIVED

Being ill-treated her whole life, Now she sits in the corner of her room, thinking what if...

She has entered a crucial age; by society's eye, she is all settled and happy in her life, has children husband, and a family. But they didn't know that there is no one she can call *Her own.*

Lived her whole life being there for everyone
Thinking about everyone,
But still, she was alone.
Had children, but they have to live their life, it's important for them,
In-laws were never hers, her own family was never hers,
She was just there all by herself.

This age brings *helplessness, self-doubt, and regret* with it. the most difficult phase for women at this age is Menopause.

Most of our population Don't know what menopause is, or what to do for women when she is going through it. Menopause is a challenge.

When a woman enters perimenopause, she goes through a lot of change, her hormones are always troubling her, mood swings, hot flashes, and whatnot!

She needs good mental support at the moment, from her children and husband, she can't describe it but is having a hard time.

At this point in her life, she's broke, but can't say it, tries to find happiness in small things, tries not to think of the past but can't help it! Remembers the time when she wished she was a boy, and then wishes the same.

Remembers, every moment she told that was unfortunate, when everyone around her had those special privileges and she didn't.

Tries to find a way to be happy with the life she is left with, but Even today she feels exactly the same as she felt when she was a kid...

She just wants to find a way to die peacefully!

All she longs for now is a chance to RE-LIVE THIS LIFE!

Enter Caption

9 798887 838717

Printed by Libri Plureos GmbH in Hamburg,
Germany